CUTHBERT MEETS THE VIKINGS

Kitten Cuthbert
Book Three

A WARM WELCOME FROM KITTEN CUTHBERT - AND BUSTER AND SHERBERT TOO!

To all our young friends — and parents and teachers…

It's great to have so many friends around the world reading about our adventures, and, if you learned about us in Kitten Cuthbert Books One and Two, you will know that we are always ready to learn new things and have lots of fun too.

By now, you will have learned a lot of new words in English and other languages, and many new ideas too.

There will quite often be new words and ideas for you in this book and that is part of the fun of learning. If a word comes up that you don't know, talk to a good teacher or your mum or dad and they will enjoy learning with you.

We really hope that you enjoy this book and discover that interesting things which happened before we were born have made a big difference to our lives today.

If you'd like to know about the next books about us, keep an eye on www.kittencuthbert.com — if you go to that website you can also click onto our very first film and Cuthbert's own shop!

Thank you again for reading about us and perhaps one day, we'll be reading about you and the great things you do.

Once you have read all three books, you will know enough to be a Professor yourself — just like Buster!

Alan Wright

"Develop your senses – especially how to see.
Realise that everything connects to everything else."
— Leonardo da Vinci, Italy, 1452-1519

"Leonardo is right, and all cats and children should do that too."
— Kitten Cuthbert, North East England, still here

First published in paperback by
Michael Terence Publishing in 2021
www.mtp.agency

Copyright © 2021 Alan Wright

Alan Wright has asserted his right to be identified
as the author of this work in accordance with the
Copyright, Designs and Patents Act 1988

ISBN 9781800941588

All rights reserved. No part of this publication may be reproduced,
stored in a retrieval system, or transmitted, in any form or by any means,
electronic, mechanical, photocopying, recording or otherwise,
without the prior permission of the publishers

Michael Terence
Publishing

*Our lovely front cover shows Buster and Cuthbert pulling the chariot and Sherbert riding
alongside Freya. She was a Viking goddess and her chariot really was pulled by two cats.
We like people, and goddesses, who like cats.*

THE REAL GODDESS FREYA WITH HER CATS

CHAPTER ONE

On one of their train trips to London, the cats were looking forward to hearing Professor Buster speaking about a subject where he had become quite an expert.

His talk was called "Which history do we believe?"

He had also written books about this as he thought it was very important to encourage children to ask difficult questions about what was really true.

As they set off on another happy train ride from Darlington, they were talking about this and Sherbert came up with a good point.

"We are lucky to have the internet these days and be able to find information very quickly."

"That's true," said Cuthbert. "My granddad said that he had to go to his local library and search a lot of books to find things out — and sometimes the information was many years old instead of being very up to date like the internet."

"That's true," said Buster, "but you have to be careful and check that what you see on the internet is true. It's best to read what a few different people say and then decide what you think is true."

"You are right," said Cuthbert. "I could put something on the internet saying that thousands of cats live on the Moon and they all go on holiday to Mars in spaceships, but it wouldn't make it true."

They all started laughing at the idea of cats in spaceships, but it was a very good thing to remember.

Buster loved the idea and decided that he was going to put it into his talk in London. He had learned that it was often good to get his audience smiling and then they listened better to what he wanted to teach them.

THE THREE CAT FRIENDS SETTING OFF ON ANOTHER GREAT TRAIN TRIP

Buster also explained to his friends that even in years long ago when there was no internet you could still find different histories, some true and some not.

"Quite often after a war for example, the people who won would write the history to make themselves look good and the losers look bad. It didn't always work like that but it usually did."

"I've been learning about a good example of that," said Cuthbert. "It was about the Vikings who lived in England many hundreds of years ago. I'll tell you all about that soon."

"Wow," squeaked Buster. "Would you believe this?"

He picked up his phone and took some pictures through the train window.

They were travelling very quickly but his camera phone did well to take a clear photo of where they had just been.

They had just passed through a lovely little town called Thirsk and Buster showed his picture of a furniture shop called Treske right next to the station.

"I'd nearly forgotten," said Buster, "but this reminds me of two lovely stories to tell in London. I love to tell my audience stories about interesting things I've seen while travelling."

"It looks like a very nice shop," said Cuthbert, "but what does it have to do with what I was saying about the Vikings?"

"Another good question," said Buster and he explained how both the shop and the town of Thirsk had Viking connections.

He told them how the word "treske" is a Viking word meaning "wood", and it sounds like our English word for trees.

"Better still, a traeskerer in Viking is a wood carver so that's a perfect name for a shop that makes wooden furniture you see."

Even today, wooden shoes called clogs are called "traesko" which means wood shoes. They are still very popular in places like Denmark and Norway where farmers and fishermen wear them to keep their feet warm and dry.

"And what you were saying about different stories in history has a good example in the town name of Thirsk, because there are three different ideas about where the name may have come from."

His friends listened carefully and heard that the name probably came from an old Viking word "thraesk" meaning a marsh, which is wet land near a river.

"We don't know for certain," said Buster. "Some people think it was a Celtic word from the Celts who lived there long before the Vikings came. They had a word "tre" meaning town and "isk" meaning a stream, tre and isk together sounds like Thirsk."

To complete his story, he told them about another idea that the name came from Thor, who was a Viking god, and "isk" for a stream.

"I love hearing all these ideas," said Cuthbert, "and I've found two brilliant words you'll like which I found when I was doing my learning about the Vikings."

"There are so many of their words which are still alive in our English language today, and one of my favourites is what we've just been looking through — a window!"

He explained that, in the Viking language, it was called a Vindauga, meaning "the eye of the wind."

"I think that's a lovely word," said Cuthbert, "because a window is just like an eye in a wall which can let the wind through when it's open."

"Ah," said Sherbert, "so why don't we call it a Vindow?"

"Another great question," said Cuthbert and he explained how the Vikings, and people in modern countries like Norway and Denmark, where the Vikings came from, say a "v" like a "w".

Getting really excited about this story now, Cuthbert explained how the Viking word for a hole in the wall had replaced the word "thirl" which the Saxon people had used before.

"So," he said, really enjoying sharing his learning, "the Saxon people who lived here once would have called the hole in your nose a "nose thirl."

"And that word is still here because we've shortened it a bit and call the holes in our noses nostrils. "

"Do you know?" asked Cuthbert. "I feel really sorry for children who don't get the fun out of learning about words and history like we do."

Buster and Sherbert made themselves comfortable as Cuthbert started his story about what the Vikings did and how much of their language and ideas are still here today.

NORTH SEA MAP

CHAPTER TWO

"Just before you tell us your Viking stories Cuthbert, can I ask you something?" said Sherbert.

"Of course," replied Cuthbert.

"Well," she said, "is it true that the Vikings were cruel and attacked people?"

"Well, that's certainly part of the story Sherbert, but only a part. They attacked Lindisfarne just up the road from where we live in north east England over a thousand years ago. I always remember it because the church there was named after Saint Cuthbert and his body was kept there. That has a big part in my story and I'll tell you more soon, but let's start with a lot of things about the Vikings that many people don't know."

"And do you remember what I said earlier about history often depends on who wrote it? This is one of those times where the losers and not the winners told the history. The people who lived on the island of Lindisfarne were good at writing but the Vikings weren't, so the story they wrote about the bad things that happened is the one we read most."

Cuthbert took one of his very deep breaths and wriggled his whiskers as he always did when he started a story. It always made Sherbert and Buster smile.

He started with the good news that he was going to take his friends on a trip to Norway and Denmark soon and show them where many of the Vikings came from.

"If you could see all the way across the North Sea from our home on the English coast, you would see a little place called Oseberg which has become really famous all over the world."

He told them how a ship had been buried there a long time ago.

Buster laughed and asked, "Why would anyone want to bury a ship?"

THE AMAZING OSEBERG SHIP IN THE OSLO MUSEUM

Cuthbert smiled too and told them that ships were very important in Viking life and burying someone famous in one was a common way of showing that they wanted to remember someone special.

The ships didn't always survive, but luckily the earth piled on top of this one kept it in good condition for over a thousand years.

"And now for some homework for you two," said Cuthbert. "I want you to practise saying the world archaeologist."

Both Buster and Sherbert concentrated hard with their eyes closed and got it just right. Buster then asked a good question.

"What is an archaeologist Cuthbert?"

That made Sherbert laugh and he told them how archaeology was about being able to dig up very old things and learn a lot about them. And, with modern gadgets, you can tell just how old they are and a lot about the people who may have been buried there too.

Buster told his friends that when he started his talk in London, he was going to begin with a picture of the Oseberg ship and, especially, the back of it.

"What's important about the back of the ship?" asked Sherbert.

"You two will love this," he replied, "it has cats on it!"

He showed them a picture of the ship which had really beautiful carving on its woodwork, including the cats.

Buster also showed them a lovely drawing of a Viking goddess Freya who drove a chariot – pulled by two cats!

"I thought the Vikings was all about men," said Sherbert, "so worshipping goddesses is good news to me. "

Buster told Sherbert that it gets even better because of the two bodies found in the ship.

THOSE CATS ON THE REAR OF THE OSEBERG SHIP

They were definitely women, and you can tell from their clothes and other clues that they were special – perhaps famous leaders or even like the royal family.

And some of the things found in the ship show that the Vikings must have travelled a lot and exchanged things with people a long way from Norway. The archaeologists found a bucket in the ship with handle decorations shaped like a buddha. They came from the Middle East countries, a very long way east of the Vikings' homes in Norway, Denmark, and Sweden.

"And now," said Cuthbert, "I want you to remember your maths and work out some numbers and dates."

"The cruel attack on Lindisfarne happened in the year 793 and that ship in Oseberg was built in 820 and buried in 834. We can tell all that from the wood and the soil."

"So just think; only a few years after being attacking warriors, they were making beautiful art."

"When we have our trip to Norway, we can visit the ship in a museum in Oslo, the capital city, and even go on a ride on a ship in the harbour which is just like the old ship would have been."

Sherbert and Buster loved these new stories and wanted to know more and more. They asked Cuthbert lots of questions about the Viking ships, why they travelled so far, and how their ideas and words are still with us.

"Right," said Cuthbert, "time for a nice cold drink and I'll tell you more."

CHAPTER THREE

Cuthbert picked up a tissue and wiped some orange juice from his lips and whiskers and said to Sherbert, "You've been very patient and polite so what is your first question please?"

"This may seem like a strange question, but I've been looking at some pictures of Norway and seeing how beautiful it is, and I wondered why the Vikings wanted to travel so much and leave their beautiful home country."

"Well done Sherbert, that's an excellent question," said Cuthbert, "and it's something really important in the Viking story."

Cuthbert explained that, like many parts of history, it's rather like completing a jigsaw puzzle – put all the pieces together and you get the full picture.

"When you two come to Norway you will see just how beautiful it is, but it had its problems for living there too."

He told them about the huge deep valleys known as fjords which lots of people like to visit every year.

"The problem was that they were very steep and made of hard rock, so there was not much land to make farms and grow food."

"That meant that it wasn't too good for animals either, so there wasn't much meat to eat. The good news for cats was that there was lots of fish in the sea and the fjords, and the Vikings were good at catching it and storing it all year round."

Cuthbert told his friends how the need to travel along the fjords and coast meant that the Vikings become really good at building boats.

"Remember that they could just use the trees around them and didn't have our modern tools, but they made brilliant ships which could travel across the North Sea – and all the way to what we now call America."

Cuthbert opened his bag and showed them a map which explained just how far the Vikings had travelled over a thousand years ago. He told them that it was even more special because many people at that time hardly ever travelled more than a few miles from their homes.

"Can you two remember what we call people who dig up very old things and learn a lot from them?"

Sherbert and Buster had huge smiles on their faces as they said together "archaeologists."

"Well done," said Cuthbert. He went on to tell them that lots of things which had been dug up from the ground proved how far the Vikings had travelled – like that buddha on the Oseberg ship and many other valuable things which had come from countries far away from places like Norway.

"The other thing you have to remember," explained Cuthbert, "is that people thought differently in those days and believed that it was not wrong to simply steal something valuable from people who owned it."

Cuthbert told his friends that there were some more new words to learn because the people who lived on Lindisfarne had built a monastery. It was also known as Holy Island because the people who lived there were monks and nuns who prayed a lot and lived a very peaceful life.

He also told them how people would give gifts to the monastery. This was often food, but also things like jewellery and gold.

Cuthbert had a little rest while he watched his young students searching these new words on their little laptops and phones.

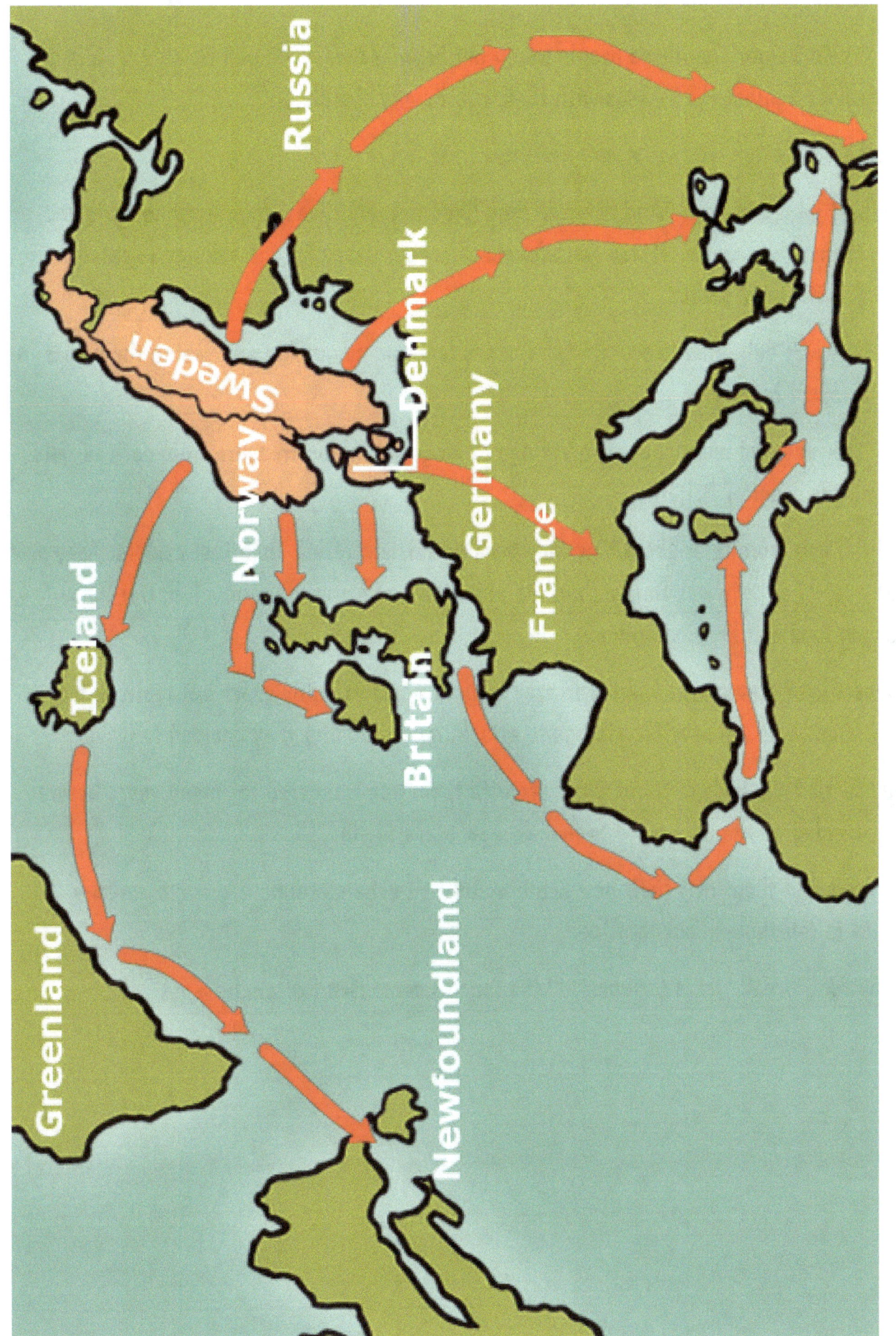

THE VIKINGS' EARLY VOYAGES

"Ah," said Buster, "so these people would not have had weapons and be able to defend themselves against the Vikings with their swords and shields."

"Well done Buster, you are a very intelligent cat."

Sherbert joined in now. "And because they liked peaceful lives, they lived on an island away from other people. It was good for that, but very easy for the Vikings to reach from the sea with their boats."

Cuthbert was delighted to see his two friends learning so quickly and seeing the pieces in the jigsaw of history.

They soon learned more about the Vikings raiding and taking treasure from easy targets around the coast of Britain.

"I'll tell you more later about how they became settlers rather than just raiders. They saw that a lot of Britain was flatter than the mountains of Norway and much better for growing food and keeping animals.

The people of Lindisfarne wanted to stay in their home of many years but realised that their island was too easy for Vikings to attack, so eventually, they decided to leave.

They carried the body of Saint Cuthbert with them and wandered for many years before they decided on the best place to make a new place to stay."

Cuthbert told them that their new home would be Durham and he had some amazing stories to tell them about that too.

"Time for a break," said Cuthbert. "Who fancies some fish for lunch?"

CUTHBERT, BUSTER AND SHERBERT ON THEIR VIKING SHIP

CHAPTER FOUR

After their lunch, Buster and Sherbert licked their lips, washed their paws, and had a little nap. It was soon time to hear more from Cuthbert and he started with a question.

"I know that you two are becoming really good at working out the meanings of words, and their history, so let me give you something to think about and I'll ask you for your answers later.

The beautiful Durham Cathedral was built over a thousand years ago by a people called the Normans, but it involved the Vikings too. Can you tell me why?"

They started to think hard and were very happy to hear more about Durham as it was close to their home in north east England.

"Well," said Cuthbert, "we should be very grateful to those monks for keeping some amazing things for us that we can still see today. As you know, they decided to leave Lindisfarne because the island was too easy for the Vikings to attack from the sea."

"When they left, over a thousand years ago, it must have been very hard work to carry something as heavy as Cuthbert's tomb. Remember, there were no cars or lorries in those days. They also brought with them a really beautiful book called the Lindisfarne Gospels which you can still see today. Without those monks, that amazing piece of work might have been lost or destroyed."

Cuthbert told his friends how the monks crossed from the island to north east England and wandered for a long time wondering where the best place was to make a forever home for the tomb of Cuthbert.

When they reached a hill in Durham, the tomb just wouldn't move any more and they took this as a sign that this was the place to stay.

They built a church there as their way of remembering Cuthbert and soon many people were coming to visit this special place.

Some years later, it was decided to replace this small church with a huge building called a cathedral.

"I like that word," said Buster "because it has a cat in it."

Cuthbert smiled at this and said, "That is true, but the real reason will need you to learn another Latin word — it's cathedra, which is Latin for chair."

It was Sherbert's turn to smile now as she said, "So a cathedral is a massive church which is special because it has a chair in it?"

"Well, sort of," replied Cuthbert, "but it was a very fine chair for the Bishop who was an important person in charge of all the churches in the area and he used the cathedral as his special place."

Cuthbert reminded them of their history lessons when they had learned that England had been invaded in 1066 by the Normans and these people built the new cathedral. They had wanted it to be one of the best in the world and they took forty years, from 1093 to 1133, to complete the building.

"They still liked the high place which the monks had found, and they built a castle just opposite the cathedral to make it easy to defend if anyone decided to attack."

Durham Cathedral has thousands of visitors from all over the world and, as well as loving the beauty of the building, people are amazed at how those brilliant people could build such a huge and strong building all those years ago without all the modern cranes and other equipment which builders use today.

The monks of Lindisfarne would be so proud to know that Saint Cuthbert's tomb is still in a special place in Durham Cathedral and many visitors like to see it and bow their heads as a sign of respect for all that Cuthbert did all those years ago.

THE BEAUTIFUL DURHAM CATHEDRAL, BUILT BY VIKINGS

"It makes me very proud to have the same name as that famous man," said Cuthbert, "but now let me go back to that question I asked you about the Normans. They built the cathedral, but why did that involve the Vikings too?"

Both Buster and Sherbert smiled because they had been doing their own homework to find out more. Buster calls it research because he's a Professor but it's really the same thing.

Buster nodded to Sherbert so that she could explain what they had found and now it was her turn to wriggle her whiskers and take a deep breath before she started.

"Well," said Sherbert, "we were looking at the map you showed us of so many places that the Vikings had travelled to, and we learned that, after starting as attackers, they had begun to live in some of these countries and eventually made friends with the people who lived there."

Sherbert explained that some people today ask the question "Why did all the Vikings disappear?"

"Of course, they didn't," pointed out Sherbert, "but they mixed with local people in those places and farmed, and traded goods, and had families together."

"Over to you Buster for the big finish," smiled Cuthbert.

Buster did his own whisker wriggle and said proudly,

"And one of those places they settled was Normandy, which is now part of France, and it was people from there who invaded England in 1066 and, most important to our story, built Durham Cathedral."

And after an even bigger whisker wriggle, he said,

"And Norman is short for North Men, which is another name for the Vikings!"

"Very well done you two," said Cuthbert proudly, because he loved them to have the same fun from learning every day as he did.

Cuthbert told them it always surprised him when some people were really silly about not liking people just because they came from another country or looked a bit different.

"In the end," he said, "all humans are part of one big family and our learning in history makes that so very clear."

"In fact," said Cuthbert, "we can do something today which would have seemed amazing to the Vikings. We can take a few drops of blood from a person and learn how your people history was put together."

"If you live today in one of these areas where the Vikings settled, there is a very strong chance that the little blood test would show you have some Viking blood."

"It's especially true of north east England where we live because the Vikings lived here for hundreds of years, but you can find the same Viking links in the blood of people from so many modern countries. It's not just Viking homelands like Norway, Denmark and Sweden, but Britain, Iceland, Greenland, Russia, America, and other places too."

People sitting near the cats on the train were listening carefully to these stories and were learning a lot.

"And the Vikings left us much more too," said Cuthbert.

"Oh," said a lady seating in the opposite seat. "Can you pause for a moment while a get another drink and then I'd love to hear more."

CHAPTER FIVE

The lady in the seat opposite picked up her coffee cup and smiled at her new cat friends, ready to hear more of Cuthbert's lovely talks about the Vikings.

The three cat friends had a glass of cool water in front of each of them, and they were especially wide glasses so that their little whiskers didn't get too wet.

"Oh," said the lady, "I thought that cats always drank milk."

"Well," said Buster, "we like a little bit of milk sometimes, but we mainly like cool water. It's very important for us, and people, because three-quarters of your body is made up of water. At home, especially when the weather is hot, we ask our people to put some ice cubes in our dishes and it keeps it beautifully cool for a long time."

The lady smiled and said, "I'm not just learning about Vikings but how simple things like water can be important in my life every day."

"Thank you," said Buster, and Cuthbert soon got back to his Viking stories.

"It's funny you should say that," he said to the lady, "because the Vikings are still important in our lives every day in so many ways."

He told them we often forget that English words we use every day have a lot of history in them.

"Speaking of every day," said Cuthbert, "the days of the week are a perfect example."

He told them that our modern words for our days go back thousands of years and often used the name of a god that people believed in.

"The easy ones are Sunday and Monday, named after the sun and moon of course.

The other days get their names from those gods I mentioned. My favourites are Wednesday, Thursday and Friday because they are named after some gods that the Vikings believed in."

Cuthbert told them how Odin, sometimes called Woden, gave his name to Woden's Day, which became Wednesday. Thor gave his name to Thursday, and our cat friend Freya is in Friday.

"When you have some spare time, it would be really interesting to learn more about these gods. Odin was very important and some stories say that he was the husband of Freya, so he probably liked cats too. It's just as well really, as he was the god of war, and it was best to have him on your side."

Sherbert looked really interested in these new stories and she said "It's amazing to think that millions of people use these words every day and don't know any of this history. I'm glad we are learning, and I'm going to teach all my friends and let them see the great fun they can have in history."

Buster smiled and said, "I'm just thinking about this because my granddad lives in Newcastle and people who live there have a lovely accent called Geordie which sounds very like modern Norwegian and Danish, and the Vikings would have loved it."

"In fact, when my Geordie granddad says Thursday it sounds like Thorsday!"

"Well done again Buster," said Cuthbert. "That's a great example and I'm going to put it in my book called The Vikings are Still with Us."

Buster gave a proud smile when he heard this.

Cuthbert said that many visitors today from Denmark and Norway come to places like Newcastle for a holiday and shopping and think that they can hear many local people speaking their language.

He told them of another good example like Buster's way of Geordies saying Thursday.

He told them that if a Geordie says that he is going home to his children, he will say, "I'm gannin yem to meen bairns."

And would you believe, a modern Danish person would say "Jeg are gannen hjem til min bairns," and a Norwegian would say, "Jeg skal hjem til barna mine."

Cuthbert soon had the cats, and the lady, practising speaking in Danish and Norwegian and they soon had it right, especially after it was explained that jeg is pronounced yi, very like the English I word.

"That's amazing," said the friendly lady. "I didn't know any of this but I'm writing it down so that I can learn more – and teach my friends!"

"Learning words from other languages is so useful," said Cuthbert, "and it can even help you to be a detective."

He told them how the Viking word "by" means a town or a city, and if you look at many town names in England it will show you where they came from.

He reminded them of a lovely trip they had made to the seaside town of Whitby, just down the coast from their home, and that town's name was a good example.

"So," said Cuthbert, "now that you know that by means town, what do you think the name means in Viking?"

"White town?" asked the lady.

"Well done," said Cuthbert, "you are learning as quickly as my cat friends," and that made her smile, and Sherbert and Buster too.

Cuthbert told them how, when the Vikings approached the town, from the sea, they saw the white cliffs and the white houses, and their name has been used for all these years.

"Wow," said Buster, "thousands of people visit Whitby every year and I bet most of them don't know about that."

Cuthbert explained that, with the knowledge they now had, they could look at so many English words and discover a lot about meanings and town names.

"Think of the Viking word for ship which is skip. And the person in charge of the ship would be the skipper. We use that word still in sport for someone who is the captain for a football or cricket team for example."

"Now that you are becoming really good at this, and wanting to know more, let me tell you how the history of England can be discovered in a few words for food."

"Do you remember how, after 1066, the Normans, who were Vikings who had moved to France, had invaded England and were in charge of the country?"

Sherbert and Buster nodded, and the lady did too.

Cuthbert explained that the rich Normans spoke French, which also has some Viking words in the language, and the poor people spoke an early kind of English.

"What does that have to do with food and history?" asked Buster.

"This is where it becomes really interesting," said Cuthbert, with that lovely smile he had on his face when he was telling a story which was particularly amazing.

"Just think of going shopping for some meat in a shop and you might be looking at beef or pork or mutton."

They are all from French words – beef, from boeuf, pork, from porc, and mutton from mouton.

"So, if you were rich and living in your big castle, they are the words you would use for the food you ate.

If you were working on the farms though, as a poor English person, you would use your own language and say cow, or pig, or sheep."

"You tell some wonderful stories Cuthbert," said Sherbert.

"And you've just reminded me that the Vikings told some great stories too. Time for another drink and then I'll tell you more."

CHAPTER SIX

Cuthbert was a very good teacher and he could tell just by looking at his listeners if they were really interested in what he was saying.

He was happy to see that Sherbert and Buster, and their lady, had their eyes wide open and were leaning slightly forward – always good signs.

Cuthbert began by explaining how the Vikings loved stories but they didn't often write them down.

"They did some of that later on," said Cuthbert, "but they must have had great memories because people would listen carefully and remember the stories exactly so that they could pass them on to others."

He told them how many of their stories tried to find a way of explaining things which they did not understand.

"People all over the world did this years ago," said Cuthbert, "and just think of something like thunder and lightning. We know what causes it through movement of air and so on, but you can understand why people without our science would think it was gods in the sky being angry with them."

Cuthbert picked out some stories which he liked, some of them quite frightening, but some very funny too.

His best funny one was the Viking story about the reason why bears have short tails.

"A clever fox told a bear that he could catch fish by dipping his long tail into a river and wait until a fish got hold of it. He could then pull his tail out quickly and then he'd have caught a fish to eat.

Of course, no fish touched the bear's tail, but he waited so long that the river froze. When he tried to pull his tail out, it snapped in the ice, and that is why bears always have short tails now."

They all laughed at this idea, and Cuthbert went on to tell them about one of the Viking's scary stories which uses a word which we use a lot today.

"They used to tell stories about trolls," said Cuthbert. "Today, it means people who do bad things on the internet, but in their stories it meant strange creatures who hid in the forests or under bridges and could jump out and frighten you."

"It's amazing that the troll word is still around today and people who use the internet will know it very well."

A NORWEGIAN TROLL SHOWING THE COUNTRY'S FLAG

"Even better," said Cuthbert, "I know that you two cats are very good at using your phones and laptops. Can you tell me what we call the way in which they can communicate with each other and lots of gadgets by sending signals without any cables?"

"Bluetooth," they said together and the lady pointed to the symbol on her laptop which showed that it used the Bluetooth system.

"Well, we all knew about that," said Buster, "but what has that to do with the Vikings?"

"It's a great story," said Cuthbert.

He told them how when the system to link phones and the rest together was made they were trying to think of a name for it.

"Luckily," said Cuthbert, "one of the team who invented it was really interested in Viking history like us, and he remembered a famous man called Harald Bluetooth who was good at bringing people together and he became King of Norway and Denmark about a thousand years ago."

"The new invention was about bringing things and people together so they thought it would be a great name."

"Why was he called Bluetooth?" asked Sherbert.

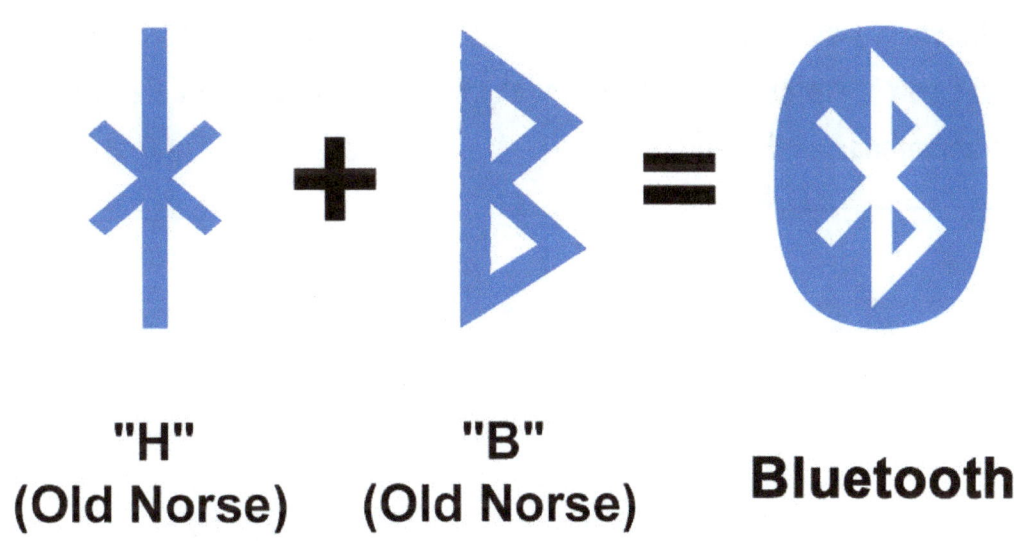

THE RUNES OF KING HARALD BLUETOOTH

"There are a few stories about that," replied Cuthbert. "Some people say he had a poorly tooth, and some say he ate too many blueberries."

"I like the blueberry story best," said Buster with a smile and a lick of his lips.

Cuthbert took out a picture from his bag and showed them it.

"These are called runes and are old Viking letters which made up words. These are the ones which spell Bluetooth and that's why you see them on millions of electronic gadgets all over the world now."

"You have so many great stories Cuthbert," said the lady, "and I know a lot more things now than when I took my seat on this train. I really look forward to sharing them with my family and friends."

"That's lovely," said Cuthbert, "and I love to give new ideas to people I meet."

"And please tell your friends that there are hundreds of pictures of Vikings with horns on their helmets and they never wore them. Someone invented them for a theatre show and the idea has stuck!"

"Do you know what Buster?" said Cuthbert. "You have become such an intelligent cat that I'd like you to be in charge of our trip to Norway and Denmark soon. I'd like you to plan all the great things to see and book our plane flights and hotels."

Buster's little chest was bursting with pride. After all his problems and bad luck as a kitten, he was now a Professor, President of the Cuthbert Club, and chief organiser of trips to the homelands of the Vikings.

HAPPY CHRISTMAS WITH THE NORWEGIAN TREE IN TRAFALGAR SQUARE, LONDON

CHAPTER SEVEN

Buster couldn't stop smiling at the thought of leading a Viking trip to Denmark and Norway with his best friends. He was determined to make it a real success which they'd always remember.

He wanted to do lots of research before the big adventure, and so he started with the expert.

"I know you are the only one of us who has been there before Cuthbert, so tell me more about what to look for."

"There's so much to enjoy," said Cuthbert, "but let me tell you two new words to learn, which will be a big help."

He told them that the first was a lovely Norwegian word "koselig" (said as kozerlee) which sounds just like our English word "cosy".

The second one was a Danish word "hygge" (said as hooger) which sounds like our English word "hug", to give someone a cuddle.

"They are such lovely words," said Cuthbert, "because they are both about being cosy and comfortable with your friends around you."

Cuthbert told Buster that there are beautiful sunny days in the summer in those countries, but it is often cold and snowy in the winter.

"It's just like those lovely winter days at our home in England when it's cold and frosty outside, and we can sit inside and have fun around a warm fire."

He told them about another lovely connection between Norway and England.

"Do you remember when we had that lovely trip to London in December and saw the beautiful Christmas tree in Trafalgar Square?"

"Oh yes, that was a great trip." agreed Sherbert and Buster.

"Well," said Cuthbert, "that tree came all the way from Norway and it's a very special present every year so that the country can say a big "thank you" for all the help that Britain gave them during the war about eighty years ago."

"You'll see lots of those big trees all over Norway and those beautiful fjords I told you about where many of the Vikings lived."

Cuthbert told them about one of his favourite places, called Gerainger Fjord.

"It's beautiful," he said, "and it has some amazing waterfalls which have a story about them."

He showed them a lovely picture of his last trip there.

He told them that those seven waterfalls were known as the Seven Sisters and just opposite them in the fjord is a single waterfall.

"They say that waterfall is a man who kept asking each of the seven sisters to marry him," smiled Cuthbert, "but he never had any luck."

"Another great place to go in Norway would be a lovely little town called Flam. I know we all love railways, and they have one there which goes up a mountain!"

"And when we go to Denmark, we can see their capital city Copenhagen which has one of the best funfairs in the world called Tivoli."

Cuthbert's little head was full of great memories of his trip and they kept on popping up.

"Oh, and not far from Copenhagen, we must visit a super place called Roskilde which has an amazing number of Viking ships which were dug up there."

"And we must make a trip to the very north of Denmark to see two little towns called Skagen and Hirtshals.

At Skagen you can stand near the beach with your feet in two separate seas. And the light there is beautiful and clear so many artists have lived there to make famous paintings.

CUTHBERT ON HIS TRIP TO GERAINGER FJORD IN NORWAY – AND SEVEN SISTERS WATERFALL.

And you can travel on the beach on a lovely little truck called the sand worm. And you can go to Hirtshals and see churches buried in the sand."

Cuthbert was speaking quickly now as he remembered so many things.

"I'll take a rest for now but wait till you go and you'll see why I love those countries so much."

Buster was scribbling all these ideas down on his little notepad and he was getting more excited by the minute.

"I'm going to use all your great ideas Cuthbert and find some of my own to plan a trip you'll never forget. We'll be just like Vikings heading off to explore."

Their train journey was nearly over and their new lady friend leaned towards her cat friends and said,

"That's been a wonderful journey. I've had so much fun and learned so much. I know that the lucky people who read your books will learn so much and want to travel too."

She gave each of them a little kiss on their heads and they all blushed under their fur.

"Well," said Buster, "I'm going to plan this great trip and, with all your help, I'm going to write a brilliant new book called Cuthbert goes to Norway and Denmark."

"And I can't wait to read it," said the lady.

ABOUT THE AUTHOR

Alan Wright was an award-winning BBC Radio and TV presenter for over 25 years and, today, has built a national reputation for his work on media training and consultancy with many large UK companies and major public bodies including the UK Fire Service and the National Health Service.

Alan has spoken professionally all over the UK and beyond and is particularly keen to see presentation skills used as a major asset for young people going into employment.

Apart from Antarctica, he has spoken on every continent and speaks on fine cruise ships around the world.

He describes the Kitten Cuthbert series as a "happy accident" inspired by his lovely rescue cat Buster. You can find out more on www.kittencuthbert.com and see Cuthbert's first film too.

More on the author on www.afterdinnerspeakeralanwright.co.uk

Alan looks forward to travelling again and meeting many of Cuthbert's friends around the world.

Alan would like to thank all who have helped with this book, including Brand Norway, Visit Denmark, LNER, all at Michael Terence Publishing, brilliant artist Chris – and especially Buster who started it all.

If you would like to follow in Cuthbert's footsteps, go to www.visitnorway.com and www.visitdenmark.com

www.ingramcontent.com/pod-product-compliance
Lightning Source LLC
LaVergne TN
LVHW081547060526
838200LV00048B/2245